# TWE...

# SEVENTEEN

Written by
Mat Coward

Illustrated by Philip Hurst

# Twenty Seventeen

Written by
Mat Coward

Illustrated by Philip Hurst

# CHAPTER ONE

When I got to the top of the hill, looked down, and saw that our street didn't exist any more, all sorts of crazy stuff flew through my head.

Like – maybe I'd got the wrong address? Nonsense, of course. I was eleven years old, and I'd lived in Hill View Terrace all my life. I knew where my own house was.

Or – maybe I'd taken a wrong turning? Impossible: I could have walked from school to home in the dark wearing a blindfold, and I still wouldn't have got lost.

OK, then – maybe ...

But by now, my brain had run out of maybes, so it decided to let me see the obvious truth. Our house – our *street* – had been bombed into dust. There was nothing left of it. From the top of the hill, I couldn't even tell where one house ended and another began.

For a couple of minutes, or maybe more, I just stood there – eyes wide, mouth open, hands and legs and teeth shaking as if I was naked in a snowstorm. I had this daft, irrelevant thought: I'm so glad we haven't got a dog. A bloke my dad used to know years ago, his house got bombed, and his dog was in it at the time. When Dad first told me that story, when I was little, I cried all night.

I stood there shivering, thinking about our non-existent dog and what a narrow escape he'd had, and then I turned and ran, faster than I'd ever run in my life. I ran right down the hill that I'd climbed up a few moments earlier, my feet slapping on the cracked tarmac, and straight through the old park, heading for Market Square. I was still shaking, and my side hurt as though someone had stuck a knife in it, but I kept running.

It had just gone four o'clock. Sometimes Mum and Dad were still at work at four. And sometimes they weren't.

It was the early summer of 2017, and the war had been going on for almost as long as I could remember. I did have some memories of the old days, of peace – I could just about remember when we had a car, for instance, and Mum used to drive it to work in London every day – but for most of my life, I'd been used to the sound of bombs falling in the distance, and always carrying a gas mask wherever you went, and being really careful about how much water you used when you washed. Stuff like that.

My mother often said, 'You can get used to anything in time', and I suppose that's true. Mum and Dad ran a fruit and veg stall in the market place, and I went to school. We lived in a two-bedroomed, terraced house – it was a bit cramped, looking back, but very comfortable – and we grew vegetables on our allotment. When the lights went out in the winter evenings, we'd read or play board games by candlelight. I'd hardly ever set foot outside Harton, my home town; neither had Mum and Dad, in the last few years.

It was an ordinary life, is what I'm saying. 'It isn't very luxurious' Mum always said, 'unless you compare it to what most people in the world have got.' We lived like millions of other families, Mum and Dad and me – no dog – in our little house, in a small town a day's walk north of London. We got by. We rarely went hungry, or suffered from the cold. It was what I knew, and it seemed like a good life to me. Good enough, anyway.

The war didn't have much to do with us, directly. Some nights, from the top of the hill, you could see the bombs falling on London, but there'd hardly ever been a direct hit on Harton. Dad once said, 'There aren't many decent targets left around here, and bombs are too expensive to waste on clapped-out old towns full of market gardeners.'

Well – it looked like he'd been wrong about that.

'Dazza!'

I started to turn round, to see where the voice was coming from, but before I could do it, I was lifted clean off the ground. He was a big man, my father.

As he swung me around and set me back on the pavement, I scanned the market place. 'Dad? Where's Mum?'

'It's all right, son, it's all right – she's safe. She's gone to the top of the hill, to try and catch you on the way home from school. We only just heard about the house.'

'I came the quick way,' I said. 'Through the park.'

'Good lad. Come on then, let's go and find your mother.'

He started marching off on his long legs, until I called him back. 'Dad – what about the stall? You can't just leave it like that.' The day's unsold stock was sitting there, in its boxes and baskets. Even the cash tin was still there, on full view. 'I'll stay here and watch the stall, while you fetch Mum, yeah?'

He turned back. 'Look, Dazza ...' He put a hand on my shoulder. 'I don't think any of this is going to matter much, now.' He must have seen the look of disbelief on my face, because he laughed and went behind the stall to pick up the cash tin. 'All right,' he said. 'You carry this. And while you're at it, take a few bits and pieces for your tea.'

Dad held open a paper bag, while I selected some of the less picked-over items from the stall: a few hazelnuts, some apples and some glasshouse strawberries. I put the paper bag into my schoolbag. At least I'd stopped shaking now, and I'd got my breath back.

As we walked, he said, 'You've seen the house, then?'

I nodded. 'The whole street. It's all gone.'

We went on in silence for a while, then Dad grinned and poked me in the side with his finger. 'Good job we haven't got a dog, eh?'

I shook my head. 'You're daft, Dad.'

What I really wanted to ask him next was – what happens now? So, to avoid that, I said, 'Why would they bomb our street?'

'I don't know, Dazza. Mistake, is my guess – they spend a lot of money on these bombs, but they don't always go where they're supposed to go. Computer error, something like that.'

'OK,' I said. 'I shouldn't take it personally, then?'

'That's it, mate! Look – there's your mum.'

My mother was hurtling down the hill

towards us, and although I wouldn't have thought I had any running left in my legs, I ran to meet her. We collided outside the Ship Inn, and she put her arms around me so tightly I was worried she might crack a rib – hers or mine.

'Oh, Darren!' She was the only person who ever called me that. 'Are you all right?'

'Course I am.' I wriggled free to avoid death by suffocation. 'Why – you weren't worried, were you?'

'Very funny. You and your dad, you're a right little double act.'

Dad had finally caught up with us. He put his arm around Mum's waist. 'There we are, love. One son and heir, safely delivered, as per instructions. We'll have to be nice to him – he's got the cash box.'

We stood there for a few minutes, and it dawned on me that my parents didn't know what to do next – where to go next. Not surprising, really: we'd usually be going home.

'Shall we go and have a look?' I said. 'You never know – there might be something worth salvaging. Some clothes, or something.'

My parents glanced at each other. Mum raised her eyebrows and Dad shrugged.

'All right,' said Mum. 'I saw the Bomb Warden on my way over. He says the site's safe enough.'

We didn't run. We walked slowly, like a family out for a stroll. I don't suppose any of us were especially keen to get there. I'd only suggested it because I couldn't think of anything else.

'When did it happen?' I asked. 'Does anyone know?'

'A bit before four,' said Dad, 'according to what people were saying down the market.'

I'd have been on my way home from school then. 'I don't understand why I didn't hear the bomb go off?'

'According to the Warden, it's a new kind of bomb called a Shaker,' my mother explained. She'd always been good at explaining things, no matter what the circumstances. Once, when

I was a kid, she caught her hand in a car door really badly and I had to call an ambulance. While we were waiting for the ambulance to arrive, she explained to me what blood was, and why so much of hers was on the floor, and what bandages were for.

'What's a Shaker?'

'It destroys buildings by agitating the microscopic particles of air between the grains of cement and brick and so on. The house collapses slowly in on itself, so the only noise it makes is a sort of quiet *whoomph*. It's supposed to be more humane, apparently, because it only affects buildings, not people.'

I tried to picture a Shaker doing its thing. 'But it'd kill you pretty well if you were *in* the building when it collapsed, wouldn't it?'

'Well, yes!' She laughed, quietly. 'I think you may have just spotted the flaw in the theory.'

# CHAPTER TWO

'This must be ours,' said Dad, stopping at a particular section of the long, slightly curved, mound of rubble. You could still tell it was supposed to be a street: it had kept its overall shape quite well.

'How do you know?' It all looked the same to me.

He pointed over the rubble, to where the top few branches of a tree were just visible.

'That's our apple tree, at the bottom of the garden.' He sighed, and Mum put her arm through his. 'I'm glad to see it still standing – I planted that before you were born.'

It was pretty obvious, this close, that there wouldn't be anything salvageable from the site. The rubble pile was only a bit taller than Dad at its highest point. There didn't seem to be a single lump bigger than a clenched fist.

Up and down the street, a few people were digging through the ruins, with spades, pickaxes and bare hands. For a moment, I couldn't think what they were looking for.

'You're all right, then?' Terry, our neighbour from two doors down, was standing behind us. 'Thank heavens for that.'

'Terry!' Mum hugged him. 'Is Tracy OK?'

'Yeah. She was at work.' He rubbed at his eyes, leaving a smear of orange dust. 'I was at the bottom of the garden, trying to fix the shed. It got blown down in that gale, couple of months ago. I only just got round to doing anything about it.' He shook his head, and made a small rasping noise at the back of his throat which might have been a laugh.

My father made a noise in his throat, too. Definitely not a laugh, this one. 'Were there many ...? Did many ... ?'

Terry shrugged. 'We don't know yet. We might never know, to be honest. But quite a few of the residents were retired folk, so ...'

'They're likely to have been home during the day,' said my mother.

And then I realised what the people were digging for. They were digging for people. I thought about that non-existent dog again, and about how lucky my family had been.

'Well, I'd best get on,' said Terry. 'Lots to do.'

'Of course. Where will you go?'

'Don't know yet. Tracy's got family in Yorkshire, if we can get there. How about you?'

'We'll sort something out,' said Dad. He shook hands with Terry, and Mum hugged him again. 'Best of luck, mate. Give our love to Tracy. Hope it all works out.'

'And you,' said Terry. He shook hands with me, and said, 'Take care of your mum and dad, Dazza.'

'I will.'

We walked off towards the Ship Inn, to see if they had a spare room for the night. 'We'll never see Terry again, will we?' I asked.

'Don't suppose so,' said Dad.

'Or any of them.'

'Well, you never know.'

I looked back at our street, at the only home I'd ever lived in. 'Couldn't we rebuild?'

'The thing is,' said Mum, 'building materials are in short supply, nationwide. And all that's left down there is dust – you saw that yourself. If there *was* anything more than dust, we'd be down there now, helping them dig.'

'Why are some people digging,' I asked, 'if it's pointless?'

Dad said, 'If *you'd* been in there, your mum and I would've been digging. That's the nearest thing to an answer I can give you, mate.'

I felt a bit sick. But maybe that was just because of all the running. 'So where *will* we go?'

'Oh, don't worry about that,' Dad said, his hand on my shoulder. 'We'll go down to your Aunty Kath's in Devon. You know what she's like – always room for one more!'

'You'll love it there,' said Mum. 'It's a real farm.'

But all I could think was that Devon was right over the other side of the country. Surely we couldn't walk all that distance? 'How will we get there?'

Neither of them replied for a while, then Dad just smiled and said, 'Well, we'll think about that tomorrow.'

Which was what he always said when he didn't know the answer to a problem.

# CHAPTER THREE

'No room at the inn,' said Dad, giving a little shrug and raising his eyebrows. Typical of him to make a joke – especially a rubbish one. But his eyes weren't smiling.

He'd rushed on ahead to check out the pub, while Mum and I walked slowly on. By the time we got there, Dad had gone into the Ship and come out again.

'Everyone had the same idea,' he said. 'And a lot of them got there quicker than us.'

Mum was rubbing his upper arm, as if he'd bruised it falling off a bike. I don't think she knew she was doing it. 'Maybe we could at least get a meal here,' she said.

I peered through the windows of the old pub at the mass of people standing around the bar, or sitting at the tables. There were even several young kids sitting on the bar billiards table, which you weren't allowed to do. The Ship was always a friendly place. On darts nights, I used to sit in the children's room at the back drinking lemonade, while my parents took turns trying to hit the board. It still looked friendly – but, despite being so crowded, it was much quieter than usual.

Dad shook his head. 'I asked about food. Ronnie says they've more or less run out of everything.' He winked at me. 'He's even managed to flog those antique pork pies at last!'

'So where *are* we going?' Mum asked. I was wondering the same thing: our beds no longer existed. They were dust. It was beginning to dawn on me – we didn't live anywhere any more.

'Don't worry,' said Dad. 'It's all sorted – the town council's opened up the old swimming pool – we can sleep there tonight. They've laid on some blankets.' He nudged me. 'Get it, Dazza? They've *laid* on some blankets.'

'Yes, Dad. Very witty.'

'Well,' said Mum, 'that'll be an adventure – sleeping in a disused swimming pool!'

She was rubbing my arm, now. I didn't stop her; she seemed to find it helpful.

The sign chiselled over the entrance to the old yellow building in the centre of town still said 'Municipal Baths'. But there hadn't been any water in the pool for as long as I could remember. Stuck to the door was a new sign, handwritten on a piece of cardboard: 'Emergency Relief Centre'.

In the foyer, there was a queue of about forty people – most of whom I knew by name or by sight – leading to a desk by the big staircase. High up on a pillar behind the desk was another sign: 'Please Register Here FIRST!'

We joined the end of the queue. Mum and Dad nodded to a few of our neighbours – our ex-neighbours – but for once, there wasn't much chatting. People just shuffled forward as the queue moved on, thinking their own thoughts. A few were crying – and not just the kids. The last time I'd been in that building was for the Christmas Panto. It seemed like a thousand years ago.

Eventually, we reached the registration desk. Mum started to speak, but an old woman behind the desk held up a hand for her to be quiet. She was still busy writing. When she'd finished, she looked up at us and said, 'Right. Name and former address, please.'

Mum gave her our details and we showed her our identity cards, then the registration woman gave us each a badge, which we were to hang around our necks on a piece of cord. 'Don't lose these,' she said. 'Your entitlements depend on them.' She pointed behind her. 'Hot drinks upstairs on the left. No smoking.'

'It's all right,' I said. 'I don't smoke.' She didn't even bother giving me a nasty look; she just went on with her work. 'She's not very friendly,' I said, as we climbed the big, stone stairs.

'Well,' said Dad, 'it's probably been a long day for her, too. I daresay she started off friendly – but the fact is, she's got a lot of people to process, no time for chitchat.'

*Process*, I thought; this morning I was a schoolboy – now I'm a person who gets processed.

The hot drink was acorn coffee – I could smell it halfway down the stairs. I reckon acorn coffee smells like sick, but a friend at school, a guy called Mark, always used to insist it was more like the aroma of a compost heap that got too wet in the winter.

Another queue. The coffee urn had been set up in the gallery, where people used to sit and watch the swimmers below. The man dishing out the hot drinks was our old postman, Corbin, a huge bloke with a huge grey beard.

'There you go,' he said. 'Three lovely mugs of cat sick – and a slice of bread and marge apiece.'

Dad and I took the bread, but Mum shook her head. 'No thanks, Corbin. I don't feel much like eating.'

'I should take it if I were you, love,' said Corbin. He had a quiet voice for such a big man. 'It's all there'll be tonight.'

'One slice of bread?' said Dad.

Corbin nodded. 'One each for tonight, and same again for breakfast. There are supposed to be some new supplies arriving late tomorrow, but for now ...'

Mum took the bread, and smiled at Corbin. 'I'll save it for later,' she said.

All the best places had been taken. The cubicles for changing in, the store rooms, the benches in the corridors; even the edges of the main pool room were occupied. That only left the pool itself – and that was filling up with people fast.

The empty pool had been boarded over long ago. It was used as a stage for shows and meetings. Mum and Dad and I, with our acorn coffee and our bread and marge, found ourselves a patch of space towards the centre of the pool, where there was still quite a bit of spare room. It seemed that people were determined to be as near the edge of the room as possible, and when we sat down I realised why – out there in the middle, I felt exposed, as if everyone was staring at me. It was like one of those dreams where you're walking down the high street naked, and everyone's staring at you.

My nose was itching, but I didn't want to scratch it in case I got a round of applause.

A man who was sitting with his wife a few metres away walked over, obviously meaning to talk to us, but then stopped just before he reached us, and sort of leant over an invisible line on the floor, smiling and raising his eyebrows. 'Hello?' he said, and I realised that he was doing the swimming pool equivalent of knocking on the door.

'Hello,' said Dad. 'Do come in.'

'Thanks, can't stop,' said the man. 'Just wanted to say – you're entitled to blankets. They're issuing them from the box office, downstairs.'

'Oh, right – many thanks,' said Dad. 'I'll get on to it.'

The man smiled, then walked back over to his own patch, content that he'd done his duty.

Twenty minutes later, Dad came back with our blankets. He was grinning, looking very pleased with himself. 'See what I've got?' He held out a tatty pack of cards.

'Oh, well done,' said Mum. 'I was wondering what we were going to do until bedtime.' I looked at my watch. Incredibly, after the longest afternoon of my life, it was still early evening.

So, we sat on our island of blankets, in the middle of a sea of floorboards, while my parents played cards and I read a book from my schoolbag. I always carried a book with me, wherever I went. Half the time, I'd carry it around all day and never even look at it – but the point was, if I had a book with me, I didn't have to stay somewhere I didn't like. I could just open up the book, and go somewhere else. The story I was reading that night was set on another planet, a million light years away.

It wasn't far enough, but it was better than nothing.

All through the evening, and well into the night, kids ran around, doors opened and closed, and people kept coming and going and holding conversations in urgent whispers that echoed off the tiled walls and bounced around the domed ceiling. Every so often the public address system crackled into life, telling us where to queue if we needed a doctor, or to book our long-distance phone call (one per Family Unit). The lights stayed on.

The night went slowly; I don't think anyone slept like a baby, even the babies.

When the loudspeaker announced breakfast, Dad and I left Mum sleeping and went to queue for our three mugs of cat sick and three slices of bread. When we got back, Mum was awake – even she couldn't sleep through the toddler at the blanket-camp next to ours, who was crying so hard that her red face looked as if it was about to explode. I had the feeling that she was almost as scared of her own noise as she was of what was going on around her.

'Breakfast is served, Ma'am,' said Dad, handing over Mum's rations. Then he clicked his fingers. 'Dazza – what happened to that bag of stuff from the stall?'

'Oh, yeah!' I'd forgotten all about it. The strawberries were only slightly squashed, and the nuts and apples were fine. Just then, the contents of that little paper bag looked like the greatest feast on Earth.

The toddler carried on screaming as the three of us stared at our bag of riches. 'I don't know,' I said. 'You feel like you ought to be sharing it out.'

'I know what you mean,' said Mum. 'But it wouldn't go far amongst so many people.'

That was true. I took the strawberries in my hand and stood up. Dad looked at Mum, then he nodded at me. I walked over to the crying girl, and put the strawberries on the blanket in front of her. She stopped screaming straight away – until she'd eaten them all; then she started up again.

'We'll eat the apples,' said Mum. 'Keep the nuts in your bag – we might be glad of them later.'

'Besides,' said Dad, 'we haven't got any nutcrackers.'

# CHAPTER FOUR

I'd never been on a train before. I didn't know many people my age who had. Public transport was scarce, and mostly reserved for official business.

There was only one railway station still operating in London. It was called Paddington, and luckily for us its lines ran west – which was where we were heading.

We never found out what delicious lunch the Emergency Relief people had in store for us, because after breakfast the public address announced that a refugee train would leave Paddington that evening and that any of us with relatives in the West Country or Wales had permission to travel on it.

Only one snag: we had to make our own way to London.

'That's got to be a seven hour march,' said Dad.

'Well then,' Mum replied. 'We'd better get started.'

We folded up our blankets, returned them to the box office, and, along with a couple of dozen of our former neighbours, set off for the city, leaving behind our home town forever.

Nothing much happened on our walk to London, except that we all half-died of hunger, thirst, exhaustion and blisters. One man took his shoes off after an hour or so, and then he couldn't get them back on to his swollen feet. Despite all that, we were feeling something close to cheerful when we arrived at Paddington. Just a few more hours, we thought, and we'd be at Aunty Kath's. Our excitement didn't last long.

'It makes sense when you think about it,' said Dad, but he didn't sound convinced, and Mum looked as if she was trying not to cry. 'They send adults and children on different trains, because – well ...'

'Because,' said Mum, 'the children's train has special markings on it, so that everyone knows what it is. There's never been a case of a children's train getting bombed, even by accident.'

'Your train leaves tomorrow morning, son. Until then, just be careful, do what the Displaced Persons Officer tells you, and we'll all meet up in Devon in a couple of days. It'll be all right, Dazza.'

'I know, Dad.'

They wrote Aunty Kath's address down for me. I gave them the cash box from the stall. They told me to keep the nuts.

As I waved my parents off on their journey west, there was one thought I couldn't get out of my mind: that if they had special children's trains so that kids wouldn't get bombed, it could only be for one reason. Because they thought the adults' trains *might* be bombed.

# CHAPTER FIVE

Even in summer it can get chilly at night. That's especially true in Victorian railway stations. Take my word for it – railway waiting rooms do not make comfortable dormitories.

More queues: leek and potato soup, this time, which was a great improvement on acorn coffee. Then, blankets again – these were pink, instead of grey.

I had never in my life spent a night away from my parents. I tried hard to convince myself that it was, after all, only for one night, and that for one night I could stand anything. But I didn't sleep much. I kept thinking that, from being a normal family, a single bomb had turned us into Tinner Ants – those tribes of people who spend their whole lives travelling around the country in old buses. It was an exaggeration, obviously, but then, being homeless is something that takes a bit of getting used to.

In the early hours, taking my blanket with me, I got up and went for a walk around the station. It was quiet – quieter than the old swimming pool had been – and I just wandered from platform to platform, reading the old notices and advertisements, some of which seemed to date back to the previous century.

It wasn't as glamorous as I'd imagined, from what Mum had told me about rail travel in the old days. I'd always thought a railway station would be colourful and bustling and full of life; people arriving and departing, to and from all parts of the country and beyond. Now the station seemed like an empty shell.

Even so, the old place smelled exciting to me. I suppose it was a dirty smell, really – the leftover aromas of machinery and dust and grease and smoke and millions of people over dozens of years. But in that still night, just before dawn, all I could smell was the scent of *possibility*. If you could just get on to a train, then you could go anywhere. Trains went faster than feet. Get on a train, and you could outrun wars.

There was one platform that curved right out of the station, following a line of track that vanished into the distance. At its far end, the platform was open to the sky, as if it had outgrown the station's roof.

I sat right at the very end, my feet
dangling off into the darkness, my blanket
around my shoulders. I didn't have a compass,
but I was sure I was looking west. I couldn't
wait for morning to come.

When I got back to the waiting room, all
the kids were awake and gathered in little
huddles around the platform, talking. Even
before I could hear what they were saying, I
could tell from their faces that they weren't just
chatting.

I saw a boy I knew vaguely from Harton,
called Asif, and asked him what was going on.

'You didn't hear the announcement?'

'No, I was – I went for a walk.'

'Well, it's bad news.'

I'd figured that out for myself. 'Is it the train?'

'It's the line,' he said, pointing in the direction from which I'd just come. 'A few miles west of here, the line has collapsed. They say it's completely destroyed.'

I felt like I'd forgotten how to breathe. *The line west.* So the trains couldn't outrun the war, after all. 'Was it bombed?'

'No, apparently it was a small landslide – you know, from the flooding.'

We hadn't had much flooding in Harton, but I knew that in many parts of the country that winter's rains had been heavier than ever before. 'The adults' train – did it ...?'

I couldn't finish my sentence, but he knew what I meant. 'There's no news,' he said. 'There are no phone masts down west, they've all been bombed long ago.'

What would my parents do, when I didn't turn up? What *could* they do? 'How long will it take to repair the line?'

He shook his head, and it was a moment before he answered. I noticed that his lower lip was bleeding from where he'd been biting it. 'Months,' he said. 'They say months, at least.'

I just couldn't take it in. Months? Surely we couldn't live in a railway station for *months*?

Eating leek and potato soup from mugs, and sleeping on benches wrapped in pink blankets.

'They'll take us to DP camps,' said Asif. He shook his head again. 'I've heard some stories about those places.'

So had I. So had everyone. 'But we're not Displaced Persons,' I said. 'We've got family. We've got somewhere to go.'

Asif laughed, but without making any noise. He seemed to think about something for a moment, then he reached into an inside pocket of his jacket and came out with four squares of chocolate. He broke off two with his teeth, and gave the other two to me. I tried to eat it slowly, but the chocolate seemed to leap down my throat. 'Thanks,' I said. 'Really, thanks a lot.'

'It's OK. Look, Dazza – what do you think a Displaced Person is? It's not a special breed of human, you know. It's just a *person* who's become *displaced*. Yeah? An ordinary person. Kids like you and me. Grandparents. Anyone. You say we've got somewhere to go, and that's true. But, think about it: that somewhere is hundreds of miles away, and we won't be able to get there for months. Face it – as of now, we are DPs. We are refugees in our own country.'

At what point did I decide to run? I'm not sure, but after my conversation with Asif, instead of waiting around with the others, swapping horror stories about DP camps, I went off wandering again through the station. And eventually, I came to an exit where there were no DPOs in sight. And I walked through it.

Looking back, I think I was simply fed up with things happening to me. I was fed up with being *processed*. So I walked out of the station, turned left, and ran.

I didn't know London at all, but I knew its

reputation. Over the years, it had been bombed more than any other British city. In theory, it was still our national capital; in practice, it was a more or less lawless place, and nobody lived there unless they had nowhere else to go.

On both sides, the streets I ran along were lined with grimy buildings several storeys high. I felt a bit trapped – back home, the buildings were smaller and the streets were broader.

After a few minutes, I heard a shout from behind me. I didn't know whether I was the target of the shout, and I didn't dare turn round to find out. I just wanted to get out of sight. Ahead of me I saw an arched doorway, surrounded by brown tiles, which had been boarded up. In the centre of the boarding was a door. It was padlocked, but the rain had warped the door frame, leaving a gap of a few centimetres.

I wriggled my fingers into that gap and tugged as hard as I could with both hands. My shoulders felt as if they were going to explode and my wrists seemed on the point of snapping, but the gap grew by a few more centimetres, until I was able to force my body into it sideways. The door snapped back into place as I squeezed through.

It was dark and cold. I took a step forward

and heard my footfall echo. I could smell dampness. With my hands held out in front of me I inched forward. My eyes slowly became accustomed and began to take advantage of the little bit of light coming through the gap in the door. There were some stairs a few metres in front of me. I couldn't imagine where they led, but I also couldn't think where else to go.

The steps spiralled downwards. They seemed unending, and I was getting tired and dizzy. It got darker the deeper I went, and I had no way of knowing how far down I'd gone. 'Maybe they just go on forever,' I thought. 'Maybe I'll just keep circling downwards for the rest of my life, until I die of starvation.'

I sat for a moment on the cold concrete, to gather my breath – if not my thoughts. I had no light, nothing to drink, and no food except for a bag of nuts in their shells. I wondered where my parents were now and whether they were worrying about me. I sighed and got up again.

'I wouldn't go any further if I were you.'

I think I screamed. I know I screamed in my head; I'm not sure if I did it out loud.

# CHAPTER SIX

'Hello ...? Who's there?' Peering around me, I couldn't see where the voice might have come from. Although, maybe ... was that a draught blowing from away to my right, or was I just imagining it?

'Don't take another step.' It was a man's voice. 'It's flooded just below you.'

There was the noise of a splash in front of me. 'What was that?'

'That was a pebble, Youth. A pebble sinking into water twenty metres deep.' Another splash. 'Twenty metres, maybe more.'

'Where are you?' I said, but, as I spoke, a light appeared over on the right hand side and a little way back up the stairs.

'Listen carefully, Youth, if you don't fancy a swim. Back up slowly, follow my voice and my torch.'

I did as he said, the sound of those splashes still in my ears. A few steps up, I saw his torchlight shining out of a hole in the wall of the stairwell, just higher than my head. In the dark, I'd walked right past it. The light disappeared. 'Where have you gone?'

'Don't panic, Youth. Put your arms up,

as far as you can, and I'll pull you through. All right?'

I tried not to cry out as my whole body weight was suspended from my wrists. It took a few moments for the man to drag me up into the hole, and by the time he'd done it both of us were breathing fast and heavily.

'You hurt your shoulder? That'll teach you to go breaking and entering.'

I suddenly realised I was trapped in a small tunnel, with a complete stranger. Just because he'd saved my life, it didn't mean he wouldn't be angry with me for trespassing. 'I'm very sorry,' I said.

'Nah, don't apologise to me. I don't own the station.'

*The station*? Had I gone through all this just to end up back at Paddington? I was about to ask him where we were, when he said, 'Now then, Youth. Who are you?'

'I'm Dazza,' I said.

'Is that right? Well, they call me Yorkie.' He turned on the torch, and as I blinked in the sudden light I caught my first glimpse of my rescuer. He was older than my dad and almost bald except for a tuft of red hair right on the top of his head. He was also rather fat; in fact, crouching down in that tunnel, he looked as round as a football.

'Right, Youth – let's get moving.' He turned
round, which took him quite a while, and
involved a lot of swearing and muttering as
various parts of his big body banged against
the walls and ceiling of the low tunnel. 'I'm too
big for this game,' he said.

I couldn't think of any polite answer to
that, so I said nothing. At last, he set off
crawling up the tunnel, and I followed him. I
had no idea where we were going; I could only
hope that we were heading west.

# CHAPTER SEVEN

'I'm glad to be out of that tunnel,' I said, as Yorkie helped me down.

He laughed. 'That wasn't a tunnel, Youth. That was just a long hole, an air vent. *That's* a tunnel.'

I turned round and looked where he was pointing. He was right – that *was* a tunnel. We were standing on a long, quite narrow platform, which at one end finished in a big, dark oval opening, from which came a wind that smelled of oil and dust.

'We're in a Tube station,' I said.

'Well, what did you think it was? A coal mine?' Yorkie was smiling as he brushed the dust off his clothes (which didn't seem to make them any cleaner), and stretched his back and neck. Not that there was much to stretch – standing up, he was indeed quite round and only just taller than me. 'You ever been in the Underground before?'

'I think so. A long time ago, when I was little. All I remember is the noise when the train was coming. A great rolling and rumbling. Like a monster waking up.'

'A monster, eh? Well, you won't have to worry about that. No trains on the Underground, not for a while now.'

'Why not?'

'Flooding,' said Yorkie. 'Bombing, what have you. No ... no trains any more.'

I was still taking it all in. Along the dark platform, there were little pools of light. Here and there, I saw movement – there were other people there.

'Where does the light come from, Yorkie?'

He pointed at the lights strung along the arched ceiling. 'Solar, of course. We've got panels Upside – street level, that is – with wires running down the old ventilation shafts.'

'Do you ... live here?'

'Ha! Yeah, only while my mansion's being redecorated.'

I took that to mean 'yes'. 'Do many people live down here?'

'Over the whole network? Hundreds, maybe thousands. Don't know, to tell you the truth – we've never taken a census. Now then, Youth, you look starved.'

'That's a coincidence,' I said, 'because I am. But I'm even thirstier than I'm hungry.'

He pointed at my schoolbag. 'Didn't you pack a canteen of water?'

'I didn't think,' I said, which was more or less true.

'All right. Let's see what we can do. You fancy a walk? You'd better do, because there are no buses down here, either.'

He jumped down from the platform on to the track. When he saw that I was hesitating, he said, 'It's all right, Youth. The rails aren't live.'

But it wasn't electricity I was worried about. I'd seen something move down there, when Yorkie had landed. 'Are there rats?'

'Rats? My God, yes. Big as dogs, some of them. But don't you worry – they'll not bother you if you don't bother them.'

That was what people used to say about the tropical mosquitoes. But my granddad, who lived on the south coast where it was warm and wet in summer, had been bitten by one. He'd been in hospital for six weeks.

'Look at it this way,' said Yorkie. 'Would you rather die of thirst or be eaten by a giant rat?'

'I don't know.'

'Tell you what, then,' he said, looping an arm around my knees and dropping me down on to the track, 'you can think about it along the way.' He wasn't a big man, but he had very strong arms.

Yorkie set off for the mouth of the tunnel, and I had no choice but to follow.

Soon I was hoping that I'd never have to find my own way out of that underground world. We went along tunnels which branched off into other tunnels; into chambers which led into other chambers; up and down shafts, some narrower than others, which eventually deposited us in new tunnels or chambers or shafts. Every now and then, we'd stop for what Yorkie called 'a little breather'. He seemed to need them as much as I did. 'Too old and too fat,' he muttered, more than once.

To take my mind off the rats – which I heard and felt a lot more often than I saw them – I got Yorkie to tell me stuff about the tunnels.

'The stations were never formally abandoned,' he explained. 'They just sort of ...

drifted into disuse, along with the rest of this poor old city. There aren't enough people living Upside any more to make it practical to run a transport system. And half the tunnels are blocked with debris.'

'From the war?'

'Mostly, yeah. Those new bombs they've got —'

'Shakers?'

He nodded. 'That's them. They play hell with the structures.' He hadn't been using the torch much – to conserve its solar cell presumably – but he switched it on now and pointed at the walls of the walkway we were in. 'See them cracks? All that'll come down one day – it's bound to.'

'What's that?' I said, using my hand on his arm to guide the torch further down the wall. 'Wow!'

'Ah, that – I'd forgotten that was there.'

How could he have *forgotten* such a thing? It was a huge mural, stretching right along the wall for about ten metres. There were dozens of different colours. I was seeing it from the wrong angle, and by weak torchlight, but even so it was beautiful.

'You need to walk along it to get the proper effect,' said Yorkie.

I soon saw what he meant: if you started at
one end, and slowly 'read' the painting as if it
were a book, it told a story. The whole thing was
a picture of London, seen from a long way off. It
began with the city all shining and undamaged
on a sunny day. Gradually, that gave way to
bomb sites and abandoned streets until, by the
time you got to the end, there was no sign of
London at all – just green fields. But right at the
very last metre of wall, there was a group of
people – men, women and children – in a field
full of wildflowers, putting up a big building,
bigger than a house; and you could just see,
around the side of the new building, a bloke
standing on a ladder. He was painting a mural.

'It's fantastic,' I said.

'Just because you live in a hole in the ground, doesn't mean you can't have something nice to look at. People'll always try to improve their surroundings, Youth, wherever they are, no matter how desperate their plight. That's human nature, that is.' Yorkie used his sleeve to brush a piece of dirt off the figure of the artist on the ladder. 'For good or ill,' he added.

'Do you know the person who painted it, Yorkie?'

'Oh yeah. I knew him.' He put a hand on my back and pushed me gently forward. 'Come on, Youth – best press on.'

During our next breather, I asked him why the government didn't do anything to save the Tube before it all fell down.

'Government?' he said. 'Ha! That's a good one.'

That particular conversation didn't seem to be going anywhere, so I changed direction. 'You haven't always lived down here?'

'Well, Youth – in a way, I have. I used to work on the Tube, you see.'

'Were you a train driver?'

'No, no – maintenance crew.'

'So that's how you know your way around so well.'

'You've got it. Mind – you can never know all of it.'

'No?'

He shook his head. 'No, no. There are hundreds of miles of it, hundreds of miles. I'm still exploring. I'll still be exploring, the day I die. That's what I was doing in that ventilation shaft, when I heard you coming down the stairs. Exploring, mapping.'

'Lucky for me,' I said, thinking of the meal to come.

'Ah, well,' said Yorkie. And we moved on again.

Occasionally we passed people – alone or

in small groups – walking in one direction or another. Yorkie would nod to some of them; some he greeted by name, or with 'All right, Youth?' or 'How do, love?'.

'Are you a Londoner?' I asked him, during a long stretch of level walking along a big tunnel.

'Not me! Londoner? No thank you – I'm from Birmingham originally.'

'Then why do they call you Yorkie?'

'Ha! Well, Youth, that's because they're Londoners and they don't know any better.'

I wanted to ask him why he hadn't gone home to Birmingham when the Tube closed down, instead of living here beneath the streets, with the rats. After thinking about it for a few minutes, the politest question I could come up with was: 'Why are you still here, Yorkie?'

It was a while before he answered, and I was worried that I'd offended him. 'I'm sorry, Yorkie – it's none of my business.'

'No, no, you're all right, Youth. It's quite simple – I've nowhere else to go. Nowhere that I'd be better off than I am here, any rate.'

I thought about the hundreds of others who lived in the Tube. 'Is that the same for everyone?'

'Some, yeah. A lot of them are ill – mentally or physically. Both, in many cases. They feel safe down here, away from the world.'

'And are they?' I asked. 'Safe?'

He put a hand on my shoulder. 'There's no such thing as safe, Youth. If you wake up in the morning and you're still alive, you've won another round. That's all.'

The little breathers became increasingly frequent, until we were spending more time sitting than we were walking. I'd given up talking – my throat was so dry from the dust that it was all I could do to grunt when Yorkie asked me if I was all right.

'Good,' he said, 'because here we are.' He pushed against a green door, and ushered me through. 'Welcome to my humming abode.'

The room was about three times the size of our old living room at home. It was brightly lit, once Yorkie switched the lights on, quite warm and dry. There was a slight smell of oil, but a stronger one of pipe tobacco. His furniture was a mixed collection: plastic chairs, like people have in their gardens, alongside dark, wooden tables and desks that might have come from a museum.

Halfway down, the room was partitioned by

blankets hanging from the ceiling. 'This is the living area, as you can see,' said Yorkie, 'and behind the curtain's my sleeping quarters.'

'Have you got a real bed?'

'I don't sleep standing up, Youth,' he replied. 'Now, bathroom's next door, and —'

'*Bathroom?*'

'Well, not exactly a bath. But there is a big sink. And a perfectly good chemical toilet. Feel free to use either, but first things first ...' He closed the door, reached up to a shelf behind it, and brought down a water purifier jug and two glasses. We each drank a glass straight off, then sipped another more slowly. It was cold and clean and wonderful.

'There,' said Yorkie. 'Feeling a bit more human?'

'Much more.'

'That's it. And if I know lads your age, as soon as you're not dying of thirst, you're starving to death. Is that right?'

I laughed. 'I could manage a morsel or two, as it goes.'

'Right then – two doors to the left, that's the kitchen.'

That first meal with Yorkie was one of the best I've ever eaten. On his tiny electric hot plate he heated up an enormous catering can of beans and sausages. Meanwhile, he told me to make some toast, spearing the bread on a long fork and holding it over the flames of what he called a brazier – which was a cut-up oil drum, as big as me, set up further down the corridor, at the base of a vent shaft.

In-between mouthfuls, Yorkie had me tell him my story. He was quite sympathetic. 'Well, Youth, there are ways of getting around the country that don't involve trains – or DP officials. But they cost money.'

'I haven't got any money.'

'There are ways of earning money,' he said. 'We'll talk about it later.'

For pudding, there was tinned mandarin segments with whipped cream from a can. While we ate that, the kettle boiled, and Yorkie made a big pot of tea – real tea, made from *real* tea bags. I drank five cups.

'You like your tea, don't you, Youth?'

'It's a lot better than cat's vomit,' I said.

He spilled some tea on his shirt. 'I should hope it is!'

It had been a while since I had felt so stuffed. Even at home, I didn't usually eat quite that much; tinned goods were fairly expensive, so we used mostly home grown veg – and cabbage doesn't fill you up the way beans and sausages do. I was having a job staying awake.

'Tell you what, Youth – there's a sleeping bag under that sofa. Why don't you get your head down for a couple of hours. You must be knackered after that long walk.'

I happily agreed; it seemed ages since I'd had a decent kip. I was just about dropping off, when something that Yorkie had said earlier popped into my head.

'Yorkie? Why do you call it your humming abode? I can't hear any humming.'

'No, not any more. But a few years back, you would've. This used to be a machine room.' He lifted the brightly coloured cloth which covered what I had thought was a large desk, revealing a shiny, squat machine with dials on it. 'This part of the Underground was used as emergency quarters during the war – World War Two, that is.'

'That's why there's a kitchen and a lavatory,' I said.

'That's it. Oh, there are all sorts down

these tunnels. There's even a complete telephone exchange.'

I sat up. 'Does it work?'

'No, no – it hasn't been used since 1945.'

'Oh.' I felt disappointed; for a moment, I'd thought I could ring Aunty Kath, and find out if my parents were there yet. But then, I didn't even know whether she had a phone, or whether the phones were working in that part of the country, or …

I woke up an hour later, feeling guilty. All that food! For all I knew, I'd just eaten Yorkie's rations for the week.

'Don't you worry about that, Youth,' he assured me. 'Food's not the problem down here.'

'What is the problem? Rats, I suppose?'

'You get used to the rats. And besides – I'm told they don't taste too bad, with a bit of barbecue sauce.'

'Leave it out, Yorkie! That's gross!'

'Why not – meat's meat, isn't it? No, the rats are mostly in the train tunnels. The rubbish worries me more. Half the garbage in London ends up underground eventually, through gratings and vents and what have you. Keeping your home clean, and free from disease – it's not easy.' He sat for a moment, with his chin on his hands, staring at nothing.

'And the asbestos dust – that's a constant worry. Lots of loose asbestos around, these days.'

'How about water?'

'Good question. Water itself isn't too difficult – there's the river, and plenty of rain. But water purifiers don't exactly grow on trees.' He smiled at me. 'But as for food – there's plenty more where that came from.'

'And where does it come from?'

'Well, Youth,' said Yorkie. 'After we've had our tea tonight, I'll show you.'

# CHAPTER EIGHT

We took a much shorter walk that evening, mostly along walkways, but detouring at one point into the largest chamber I'd seen underground. The size of a football pitch, it was also a high room, its ceiling invisible in the gloom.

Here and there, I saw the glow of campfires. There were tents of various sizes and colours and huts made of corrugated iron, or wood, or brick, freestanding or leaning against the walls.

I was about to ask Yorkie how many people lived in that one great room, when a movement above caught my eye. 'Are there birds living up there?'

Yorkie didn't answer: he didn't need to. I heard the rasp of a match, and in its brief illumination I saw a man, up by the ceiling, lighting a pipe. He was on a rafter no wider than a school desk, and he was crouching rather than sitting – his feet on the rafter, but his backside a few centimetres above it. *Perching* was the word that came to mind.

Yorkie shrugged. 'Some folk seem to prefer

spending their time up there, rather than down here. Men, mostly. Who knows why?' He smiled. 'Maybe his wife doesn't like him smoking, eh?'

Now I knew to look for them, I could see more bird-men on the rafters, perching and shuffling. All of them on their own. A couple of them, I was sure, were fast asleep. 'But, Yorkie – if they fell ...'

'Oh yeah, it'd kill 'em. Still, you don't have to go up there to be killed – there are plenty of dangers at ground level, you know.'

I didn't have time to worry about that. Yorkie was in a hurry, and we marched on.

The street we stood in, twenty minutes later, just as dusk was falling, didn't look badly damaged – but it did look abandoned. It was obviously a shopping street, but many of the shops were boarded up, and all of them looked half-empty behind their dirt-encrusted windows.

There was a small supermarket a few doors down with a poster in the window advertising frozen chickens. The poster had a picture of Father Christmas on it. 'Is that where you get your food, Yorkie?'

'Used to be one of the places – it's more or less gutted now.'

There was no noise at all, and nothing moved. 'Does *anyone* still live in London? Upside, I mean.'

'Oh yes, but not many in the city centre. The further out you go, the more people you find. So I stick to the central areas, mostly.'

'Why? Wouldn't you find more people to trade with if —'

'The trading comes later, Youth. At this end of the operation, what we're engaged in is more what you'd call recycling. You know about recycling? They taught you all that at school? Well, there's a good living to be made in recycling. Of course, most of the obvious stuff's already gone. You won't find a spare radio in the whole of London, I guarantee you that.'

'So what do you recycle?'

'You have to be imaginative,' he said. 'For instance – the town where you lived, did you have a local paper?'

'Yes, though it was only a couple of pages. Because of the paper shortage.'

'Right. Well, paper's not really my department. Too heavy you see, no transport. But supposing a widget went bang on their printing press —'

I interrupted. 'What's a widget?'

'It's a thing that goes bang on printing presses, Youth. Now, a widget's only a small thing, easily carried, and I know where I can lay my hands on such an item which is no longer in use.'

'So you recycle it?'

'That's it, Youth! What do you think – better than letting things rust and rot, isn't it?'

'I suppose it is,' I said, but I was frowning. I'm not an idiot – I knew what Yorkie was saying. He was telling me that he took things, from abandoned shops, businesses – even homes, probably. Took things as in *nicked* them. It was definitely stealing – they weren't his, and if you take something that isn't yours, that's stealing.

On the other hand – who *did* all this stuff belong to? The tins of mandarins and the printer's widgets? No one who was around to claim it, that's for sure.

Yorkie gave me a long look. 'What's the matter, Youth? Don't you have recycling where you come from?'

We did, of course. It was against the law to chuck anything on the town tip without permission. 'Yeah ... but the council runs it.'

'See, we don't have a council here. So we have to run it ourselves.'

He was waiting for me to say something. 'All right,' I said. I didn't want him to think I was disapproving of him. He'd been very generous to me, and besides, 'People have to make a living', which was one of my dad's favourite phrases. 'What are we recycling tonight, then?'

Yorkie grinned and slapped me on the shoulder. I'd have been happier if he hadn't, really, because that shoulder was still sore from where I'd used it to break into the Tube station – which, now I came to think of it, was almost certainly against the law.

'Good lad! Follow me.'

Upside was almost as confusing as the Underground. Yorkie led me along streets and down side alleys and up short cuts, until we came to a half-demolished house.

'Now, have to be a bit careful here, Youth.'

'Are we going in there?'

'We're going *through* there. Tread carefully, stick close, and if anything happens – just get out as quick as you can. You understand? Don't bother about me, I'll be fine.'

In fact, although the place looked as if it might come down any moment, it only took us a moment to walk in the front door, out the back, and over a brick wall at the rear.

'Wow,' I said, looking around. 'It's a jungle!'

'It's a car park,' said Yorkie. 'Used to be, anyway, when there were enough cars around to need one.' He stamped his foot. 'See? Underneath it's tarmac. But a lot of these plants – buddleia, for instance, that stuff there – they'll grow in any tiny crack, if they're left to get on with it.'

It still looked like a jungle to me. Plants covered almost every piece of ground, and the tallest of them wrestled with each other above our heads. Insects buzzed at the flowers, and there were rustling noises around our feet.

We pushed our way through the tangled
vegetation, half-crouching, and before long
we were facing the front of another shop.
The daylight was fading, and it was dark
anyway in the shadow of that jungle, but as
far as I could see this shop was intact. Even
the plastic sign was still in one piece:
'Pharmacist'.

Yorkie rubbed his hands together.
'There she is. Now, Youth, you need to make
yourself some money, to get you on your
way west. Right? Well, here's your chance.
This place – I don't think anyone
remembers it's here except me. It's hidden

by broken down buildings and overgrown car parks on both sides. If I'm right, it's never been touched by another recycler – and it's full of gold!'

'*Gold*?'

'Better than gold! *Medicines*. Aspirins, anti-diarrhoea tablets, mosquito patches, asthma inhalers, water purifiers – you name it. There's nothing more valuable to a recycler than medicines.'

I could see the sense in that. Back home, a small bottle of antiseptic was worth seven or eight pounds of spuds. 'But why have you never ... *recycled* from it before?'

Yorkie gave me an odd little smile. He patted me on the back, without looking at me. 'See, that's simple, Youth – I can't get in there. But I think *you* can.'

He was right. A man shaped like a gigantic football could never have wriggled through that tiny window in the staff lavatory – even after he'd smashed all the glass out of it.

'Mind yourself on the shards, Youth!'

'I'm all right.'

'Just be careful. I can't send you home to your mum with fingers missing.'

He stood outside with a big sack, while I passed stuff through to him, according to his instructions. It was a laborious business, as I could only climb up on to the cistern to the window carrying small amounts at a time. After a dozen trips, Yorkie called, 'That'll do. We'll come back for more tomorrow.'

But we never did.

I was feeling cheerful as we fought our way back through the jungle. A few recycling jobs like this, and maybe I'd have enough money to get me to Devon. For the first time since Paddington, it seemed as if I was again heading towards my parents.

I spotted the patrol a couple of seconds after it spotted us. We were only about five minutes from being safely back underground. Yorkie, struggling under the weight of the recycling sack, was several paces behind me.

'Yorkie!' I yelled, pointing at the two

soldiers as they walked steadily down the street towards us.

He looked up, and his shoulders slumped. 'Oh, hell! I never thought they'd be … if I'd thought this might happen, I'd never have … I'm so sorry, Youth. I'm so sorry. Listen – you just follow my lead and everything'll be all right. Understand?'

'Should we run?'

'*No*! Just follow my lead.'

One of the soldiers stood a few metres away, covering us with his rifle, while the other strode up to Yorkie. 'Let's see what you've got in that bag then, Fatty.' Yorkie didn't resist, as the man tipped out the contents of the sack. 'Got receipts for this lot, have you?'

Yorkie said nothing.

'Thought not. Right then, you're both under arrest for looting, under Section 17 of the Emergency —'

'What do you mean "both"?' Yorkie interrupted. 'I've never seen this kid before in my life.'

'Is that right?' The soldier sneered. 'Then how come he called out your name, just now? I heard him yell, "Yorkie".'

Yorkie spread his hands and smiled. 'There you are, then. Proves it! You're a Yorkshireman yourself, from your accent. Am I right?'

'Might be.'

'Well, do I sound like a Yorkie to you?'

The soldier looked at me, then back at Yorkie. 'You sound like a Brummie,' he said.

'And so I am. I reckon the boy's an orphan. He was just asking me for directions. Why don't you search him?'

The soldier patted me down, ordered me to turn out my pockets, and finally pawed through my schoolbag. 'What are these?'

Out of the corner of my eye, I saw Yorkie start in alarm. But he smiled to himself, and relaxed, when I said, 'Nuts. They're for my dinner.'

The soldier gave me my bag back. 'Is that right, you're an orphan?'

'I – yes, sir.' I hated saying it, as if the words might make it true. For all I knew, it was already true.

His voice softened a little. 'Got lost, have you?'

'Yes, sir.'

'I was telling him how to get to the nearest DP centre,' Yorkie said.

'Shut it, Fatty.' The soldier chewed his lip for a while. Then he nodded. 'Private!' he yelled.

'Sir?' said the other soldier.

'This one's a DP – take him back to the jeep. I'll walk the fat one back myself.'

'Sir!' The junior soldier came forward and grabbed hold of my arm. As he marched me away, I looked over my shoulder at Yorkie. He gave me a tiny nod – so small, you wouldn't have seen it if you weren't looking for it.

'What'll happen to – to that man?' I asked.

'Who? Fatty?' the soldier answered. 'Well, what do you think happens to someone caught looting during wartime? Stealing from the dead! Don't you worry, kid – he'll get what he deserves.'

And with his spare hand, he made his fingers into the shape of a gun, aimed them at his head, and said, 'Bang!'

# CHAPTER NINE

I wasn't aware of much during the next few hours. I know I was taken somewhere, and *processed*; and from there I was taken somewhere else, and processed some more, and so on. I answered when I was spoken to and I ate what was put in front of me and I slept when my eyes would stay closed, but most of the time I thought about Yorkie and what might be happening to him *right at that moment* – and how it had only happened because he was trying to get me enough money to head west.

And now here I was, heading north instead.

I don't remember much about the boat trip to Scotland, except meeting Una.

There were hundreds of children and teenagers on board, and about ten DPOs – Displaced Persons Officers. Half the DPs were throwing up, half were racing around, enjoying their first journey by sea; I was sitting on deck in the sun, leaning against some boaty-bit that I didn't bother to learn the name of. I didn't feel sick. I couldn't be bothered to feel sick.

One of the DPOs was patrolling the deck, which mostly involved swaggering up and down in front of a group of teenage girls. He was only a couple of years older than them, and he probably thought he looked pretty cool in his uniform tunic. Perhaps he did, until he slipped on a seagull dropping, and landed on his backside on the deck. He appeared to bounce slightly, which was probably very painful – but was also rather funny.

I tried not to laugh – for all sorts of reasons – but from behind me came the noise of someone laughing hard. I looked round and saw a girl of about my own age, rocking backwards and forwards on her heels, with both hands over her mouth. I couldn't help smiling, and she smiled back, and I felt half a ton lighter. Thing is, I'm not a whinger by nature – but I really don't like being alone.

Once off the boat, we had a cross-country hike during which dozens of DPs and at least one DPO collapsed along the way from dehydration and exhaustion – until we arrived at somewhere that wasn't anywhere, as far as I could see. It was just another stretch of empty countryside, same as the ones we'd spent all day walking through. The only difference was the tents, which stretched as far as you could see, off towards the hills in the distance. They were all the same colour and size – beige and small – which made for a depressing scene.

At one end of the camp there was a small village of prefab buildings. We queued in a long hut full of benches for a brunch of bread, cheese, one pickled onion and one cup of tea. Then we queued in another hut, called the Quartermaster's, to be issued with a tent, a tin mug and a toothbrush.

'You can't have anything that doesn't begin with T,' Una whispered.

'In that case,' I replied, 'when do we get the toilet paper?'

No one told us where to put our tents, so we found ourselves a reasonably level piece of ground and then tried to figure out the tent instructions – which were in pictures, not words, presumably because so many native languages existed amongst the DPs.

After an hour of frustration, Una said, 'I reckon the *pictures* are in a foreign language.'

A boy a couple of years older than us saw us struggling and came over to show us how to do it. He introduced himself as Hal and then pointed at my schoolbag. 'What you got in there, then – anything to trade?'

I showed him the nuts I'd carried all the way from Harton. 'Don't suppose you've got a nutcracker?'

'No problem.' He went away for a few minutes, and when he came back he was carrying two stones, one flat and one rounded. He smashed the nuts open, and the three of us ate them. In a way, I was sorry to see them go – they'd been a reminder of my old life. Hal ate quickly, with his hand close to his face, hunched over and looking around him constantly.

'What else?' he said when he'd finished. 'Schoolbooks? Yeah, they might be worth something. Ah – a space novel! What do you

want for that?' I told him it wasn't for sale, but he shook his head. 'Listen, mate, if you've got something to trade, trade it while you can. Two girls last week ended up in the hospital hut – knifed each other fighting over a stick of chewing gum.'

'Suppose Dazza did want to trade the book,' said Una. 'What could you give for it?'

'Could find you a better spot for your tents. Nearer the lavs, say – but not too near.'

I told him I'd think about it. That night, while I slept, the schoolbag was stolen from my tent.

Queuing. That was pretty much all we did at Green Glen Juvenile Refugee Facility.

There were about two thousand DPs in the camp, all children. Some were foreign refugees whose parents hadn't made it this far – drowned in small boats, shot dead in the channel tunnel, or taken by disease in the gigantic reception camps along the coast of the English Channel. Some DPs were 'orphans' like me – and lots of them were real orphans, like Una. 'A bio-attack,' she said, when I asked her about her parents once. And that was all she said on that subject, ever.

We queued for food, for water, for doctors.

The rest of the time we sat in our tents. Or outside our tents. You could tell, we reckoned, the ones who'd been there longest; they sat all day staring at nothing, not talking to anyone, and occasionally joining queues just for fun, or maybe out of habit.

One group of teenagers – we guessed they were Afghans – had a tatty cricket ball, and a bat carved from what looked like a piece of driftwood. They spent almost all day, from sunrise to sunset, playing 27-a-side cricket. (Una said it was 27-a-side, but I think she was guessing). The cricketers let me and Una field, but we never got a turn at batting or bowling.

Never having quite enough to eat or drink, the discomfort of living in tents, the dirt, and the constant fear of occasional violence – all these we could live with. But there was one thing we just couldn't stand: if it was possible to die of boredom, they'd have been burying us by the end of our third day. 'I never thought I'd miss school,' I said, 'but ...'

'I know what you mean.' Una stood up. 'Come on, we can't just sit here and turn into vegetables.'

In the hut marked 'Administrator's Office' we asked a woman with a worried face, who looked almost as thin as most of the DPs, if she could give us something to do.

She looked us over. 'Bored, eh? Well ... are you two fit?' We nodded enthusiastically. 'Tell you what, then – I might have a job for you. It'd mean better rations and no more queuing.'

'We'll take it,' I said.

'Hold on,' said Una. 'What is this job?'

'Working at the Water Recycling Plant.'

'We'll take it,' I said again.

Una frowned at me, and started to speak, but the administrator smiled for the first time and said: 'Well done. Now – I just need you to sign a couple of forms ...'

We were driven to the plant the next morning in a solar buggy. It was a kilometre or so from the camp, and was (explained the driver, an Irish DP in his late teens) the only reason the camp could continue to exist. 'You couldn't feed that many mouths on charitable aid and the camp's vegetable gardens. But the recycling plant earns proper money. Without it ... well, we'd all have starved long ago.'

'Why is recycled water so valuable?' I asked. Una wasn't saying much. The previous night she'd said she had a nasty feeling about all this, and had only come because I'd begged her to.

'Two thirds of the world's population doesn't have regular access to clean drinking water,' said the driver.

'Why?'

'Climate change, population growth, industrial expansion, poor management of resources. Lots of reasons. They've known it was coming since the 1990s – just never actually did anything about it.'

He sounded bitter, and I wondered what his personal story was. 'It's the biggest single cause of refugees leaving home. *Millions* of them. Rich countries like ours import water – with or without the cooperation of the people in the exporting countries. But there's still not enough to go around, so nations fight each other for control of what there is. So if you can reclaim used water, you're less dependent on imports.'

He looked at me in the mirror and laughed. 'Did you never wonder what this endless war was all about?'

I shrugged, a bit embarrassed. 'Not really. It's just – you know, always been there. Until my house got bombed, it didn't seem to affect me that much.'

'Take a tip from me, kid. *Never* pass up an opportunity to find out what's going on. The more you know, the less they can take advantage of you.'

When we reached the plant, he shook hands with us, quite formally, and said, 'Good luck.'

'Did you see the look on his face?' said Una, when the driver had gone. 'Like someone saying goodbye to a dying relative. I *told* you this was dodgy.'

I couldn't argue. Deep in my guts, I was beginning to feel the same way.

# CHAPTER TEN

'Skimmers,' they called us. The Water Recycling Plant was a low, sprawling, concrete building, made up of dozens of large rooms. There were big water pipes at each end of the building – incoming and outgoing, we assumed.

The skimming room consisted of a tank the size and depth of a swimming pool (indeed, everyone referred to it as 'the pool'), fed by a pipe connected to what was called 'the receiving room'.

The pool was surrounded by scaffolding, just above water level, and that's where the skimmers knelt or crouched – about twenty of us, mostly teenagers, spaced a few metres apart all the way around.

At the beginning of the shift, the pool would fill with old water – called 'mire' in the jargon of that place – which was dark; you couldn't see through it at all. Its surface was covered with foamy grey scum, known as 'spume'. We were equipped with flat nets on the end of long poles, and our job was to skim off the spume and deposit it in the open drains behind us. Once the mire was skimmed it passed along the pipe into 'the salting room' where it would undergo various biological cleansing processes.

The work was a strain on the arms and on the back – not to mention the knees and, come to think of it, every other part of the body. But it definitely beat sitting around in a tent waiting for the next exciting queue to form.

The worst thing was the smell. It was a thick, gagging stink of decay, and the face masks we wore did nothing to keep it out. Nor did the goggles prevent our eyes from watering non-stop – either from the smell, or from the harsh, cutting gases that rose heavily from the mire and lodged themselves in our sinuses and lungs.

The shift only lasted four hours – we'd been told the working day was short because the work was so hard – but even so, by the end of it I felt quite drowsy and had to keep blinking so as not to nod off. I was more than ready for lunch. As promised, the rations in the plant were much better than in the camp: a stew of meat and vegetables, followed by a slice of heavy pudding with custard. Unfortunately – despite the thick rubber gauntlets we wore while skimming, and the black, medicinal soap in the washroom – I could smell the mire all over my hands and taste it in every mouthful I ate.

We all ate in silence, too hungry to talk, but once we'd finished (which didn't take long) a girl sitting opposite me and Una said, 'That's one good thing about this place – you won't starve to death.' I couldn't tell how old she was, or what she looked like, because we were all still wearing our floppy skimmers' hats, like lumps of uncooked dough, which covered our hair and foreheads.

'No,' I agreed. 'Good nosh.'

'So what are the bad things about this place?' asked Una.

'For a start, you'll never get that stench out

of your hair or the taste out of your mouth.'

'Surely you get used to it?' I said.

The girl shrugged, as if she'd like to agree, but couldn't.

'I pity whoever ends up drinking the stuff,' said Una.

The girl laughed. 'No one drinks it – it's recycled for industrial use. It just has to be clean enough not to clog up machinery, or to catch fire if a spark hits it.'

'Any other horrors we should know about?' said Una.

'Well ...' The girl hesitated. 'Sometimes people die.'

Una and I looked at each other. 'What do you mean?' Una said.

'It's the fumes,' said the girl, leaning towards us over the table. 'They make you sleepy, and sometimes – well, people just ... topple in.'

Una went pale and put her hand over her mouth. She tried to catch my eye, but I looked away.

That evening, playing a board game in the dayroom, we saw the same girl without her hat. I only recognised her because she said 'Hi'. She was completely bald.

Sceptical as she was, even Una had to admit that our new lodgings were a step up from the tents of Green Glen. We slept in dormitories – boys in one wing, girls in the other – in real beds, with real lavatories and mini-showers at the end of the corridors. There was a walled area of grass and bushes, known as the garden, where all the DPs were allowed to play, or sit in the sun, during the afternoons.

Most important of all, we got three decent meals a day. Breakfast was porridge with real milk and a splodge of jam, washed down with real tea, and the evening meal was usually a dense soup with lots of bread.

True, it was difficult to stop thinking about what the bald girl had said. And it was impossible not to notice that about half the DPs in the place either had no hair, or very little. Still, hard work in exchange for warm beds and hot food didn't seem such a bad deal. I reckoned we'd do a couple of weeks at the plant, to get ourselves rested and fed, and then think about finding a way of travelling to Aunty Kath's. I mentioned this to Una one morning at breakfast, and to my surprise she went quiet and didn't respond to any of my usual attempts at making her laugh. I had to drag it out of her, but eventually she told me what was wrong.

'I'm not sure you're allowed to just *leave*, Dazza. Remember, you're legally an orphan, as well as a DP, and you signed papers at the camp agreeing to be transferred to this place.'

I hadn't thought of that. 'You mean they'd keep us here against our will?'

She gave me a sad smile, and said, 'That's the other thing. You keep saying *us*. But I haven't got any aunts in Devon. Or anywhere else.'

'Don't be daft! Of course you're coming to Devon with me – my Aunty Kath's always got room for one more. She's famous for it.'

'Oh, Dazza – that's a really kind thought, but —'

'It's not just a *thought*, Una! It's what we're going to do. And we can't wait too long, either, or my parents'll think I'm dead.'

'I'm sure your parents will find out where you are eventually. It may take a while, but they'll get in touch with the government, and then —'

I shook my head. I *had* been thinking about this, ever since London. 'I don't believe there is any government any more. There are just lots of little bits of government all over the country, and they're not properly joined up. No, the only way I'm ever going to get home is by doing it myself. And I'm not leaving you here to go bald.'

She laughed at that, at least.

It was all talk, to be honest. I didn't have the first idea how to make it happen, and it was quite obvious that Una didn't believe for a minute that she was coming with me – always supposing I was going anywhere.

Two hours into the shift, all that changed.

To put it mildly, skimming was a job you could do without using your whole brain. I'd throw the pole out over the mire, letting it slide through my hands until I caught it at the point of balance, then I'd perform a kind of sideways twist of the wrist. The net would load up with spume, and I'd swing it back up towards the scaffolding and over to the drains. I'd tip the pole, tap it a few times to clear any cling-ons, then throw it out over the pool again – all the time, my mind elsewhere.

It was while I was doing the tipping and tapping bit that I had the feeling something was wrong, as if I'd seen something, but hadn't properly registered it. I looked to my right, where Una was stationed: no, she was fine, working away, whistling.

I looked over at the boy working to my left – and immediately saw what it was that had caught my attention. The boy's pole wasn't moving. He seemed to be just sitting there, his arms on the low railing in front of him, as if he were enjoying the view. Then I saw him sway slightly, and I remembered what the bald girl had said. The kid was unconscious ...

There was no time to call out or to get help. I started running towards him and immediately tripped over my pole. Angrily, I threw it away and went on. I was almost within reach when his weight suddenly shifted forwards and he began to topple, very slowly, into the pool. I screamed and dived towards him, managing to get one hand on to one of his calves. I'll never forget that feeling, as my gauntleted fingers slid along his ankle. I was

lying flat out on the scaffolding, and the truth is I didn't have a chance in hell of holding on. If my grip had held, I'd probably have gone in with him. A falling body weighs a lot.

The splash as he entered the mire seemed a long time in coming. I was left lying on the scaffolding, with the boy's shoe and sock in my right hand.

They cancelled the rest of the shift, and we all went off for a very quiet lunch. We managed to eat it all, though; when you're hungry, nothing else comes first.

In a corner of the dayroom, I said to Una, 'We're getting out. And I don't mean soon, I mean today.'

She nodded. What had seemed like a dream a few hours before, was a necessity now. We both understood that.

It was Una who came up with the escape plan. I was full of stuff like waiting until dark, then tying our blankets together and abseiling out of the window. She waited until I'd finished, then she said, 'Or, we could just walk out.'

Her idea made sense. An accident at the plant was bound to throw everything into chaos, at least for a few hours. The plant managers and the DPOs would be too busy to keep a close eye on us lot. We'd go out to the garden as normal for our exercise period, make sure no one was watching, and then climb over the wall … and run for it.

That was very nearly how it went, too.

After the morning's tragedy, the garden wasn't busy that afternoon – as we'd hoped. There was only one DPO on duty, and she couldn't be everywhere at once. Disappearing from her view wasn't hard, nor was scaling the wall; Una boosted me up, then I pulled her after me. Jumping down on the other side of the wall wasn't hard – though it did take a bit of determination. Walls are much higher when you're on top of them than they are when you look at them from the ground.

I set off running, and had gone a good few metres before I realised Una wasn't with me. I looked back: she was sitting at the base of the wall, taking her left shoe off.

I ran back. 'What are you *doing*?'

When she looked up, I could see her face was wet. 'I've done my ankle in, Dazza. I think it's sprained, I can't stand properly.'

'Oh no …'

She looked up at me for a moment, then she swallowed and said, 'You'd best get going.'

I was almost angry with her for saying that.

It made me think of Yorkie, for some reason. 'You have to do things,' I said.

She shook her head. 'What are you talking about?'

'In life. You have to do things, not just have things done to you.' I helped her to her feet – foot, anyway – and put one of her arms around my neck.

'Look, Dazza, this isn't —'

'We won't be missed until teatime,' I said. 'We'll be lost in some forest by then. Come on, hop!'

'What forest? Where are we going?'

'South,' I said. 'South and west – that's all I know.'

# CHAPTER ELEVEN

'We can't walk all the way to Devon,' Una whispered, 'with no food, no water, and only three legs between us.'

'I know, but —'

'Dazza, we don't even know what *part* of Scotland we're in – for all we know, we could be at the northernmost tip of Britain.'

We were arguing about the Tinner Ants – Una reckoned they were our best bet for getting south, but I wasn't so keen. 'How do you know they'd even let us join them? You know what people say about them.'

'Honestly,' she said, 'I'm sure that's just a myth. You don't seriously think they eat children?'

'I'm not an idiot, Una! All I'm saying is they live in vast tribes, travelling the country in great caravans or solar buses, living off the land. They're outlaws.'

'Like us, you mean? Look, if we try walking on the main roads a patrol will pick us up and take us back. And even if we're not caught —'

'I know,' I said. 'No water, no food, three legs.'

'Anyway – I can't see a great caravan, can you? Just two buses.'

Fact was, I couldn't think of any better plan. It was getting dark. We were crouched in some woods, overlooking a minor road, watching five adults and six children sitting outside their buses, cooking a meal over a small fire. The smell was driving me mad.

'Come on,' said Una. 'If we're going to do it, let's do it before they've finished eating.'

Slowly we emerged from the cover of the trees. We'd only gone a couple of paces when one of the men – a tall bloke with long hair – leapt to his feet, holding a thick length of wood in both hands. 'Who the hell are you?'

'We're ... lost,' said Una. 'And I'm injured.'

The man took a step towards us. 'Clear off!'

One of the two women stood up and beckoned to us. 'They're only kids, Leo. Come and sit down.'

We did as we were told. The Tinner Ant children stared at us. One of the three men, who was much older than the other two, handed us mugs of cold water. We thanked him and gulped the water down. It was sweet and sharp, and it scraped all the dust from inside our throats. The man with the big stick, Leo, glared at us from across the fire.

The third man, who was bald with an enormous moustache, said, 'Lost, eh? Where you trying to get to?'

'Devon.'

'Well,' he said, 'we're going to the West Country —'

Leo was on his feet again. 'We haven't got room for *passengers*, Gene!'

'Don't be so paranoid, Leo. Another pair of hands is always welcome.'

'We don't mind hard work,' said Una, and I nodded firmly.

The second woman, who was sitting by Leo, spoke for the first time. 'What sort of work are *you* going to do?' she asked Una. 'I saw you limping just now.'

'Now, come on,' said the friendly woman. 'We can at least give them a meal and a bed for the night. We'll talk about the rest in the morning. All right?'

'You can do what you want in your own bus,' said Leo. But he looked unhappy about it.

While we ate – fish and potatoes baked in the fire – we introduced ourselves properly. There were two Ant families in two buses: Gene and Marie Ealham, and Jan and Leo Arnold.

I never did sort out the children – four girls and two boys all younger than me – who seemed to be in and out of each other's buses at will. The old man was Marie's father, Harry. After dinner, he offered to show me their bus. He'd been a Tinner Ant most of his life and his children and grandchildren had been born into it.

The bus seemed bigger inside than it was outside, even though it was so full with all sorts of gear held to the walls by straps, and loads of books and old photo albums. It had different 'rooms' divided by curtains. In the sleeping area there were bunk beds which folded up against the wall during the day. It was as if someone had taken a normal house and trimmed it down to fit in a big box.

'It must be a great life,' I said.

'Used to be. There was a time when there were thousands of us all over the country. We even had our own parliament. There are only a few still following the old ways now.'

'Why?'

'Reasons.' He slapped the side of the bus. 'For one thing, you can't get the parts. We thought these solar jobs'd be the making of us when they first came out – no fuel costs, you see – and so they were for a while.'

'What happened?'

'The war happened, son. The solar panels are fine – they'll last forever, more or less – plenty of power there to boil water, run a shower, a music system, lights, whatever you like. But all the power on earth don't matter once the engine's had its day – which this one has, pretty much.'

I was still imagining an Ant bus, sucking energy from the sky, barrelling along country roads, free as a wild horse. 'How fast can it go?'

He laughed. 'Depends how strong you are.' In the morning, I found out what he meant.

Leo and Marie had a loud argument after breakfast – about us, obviously. Leo was dead against giving rides to strangers. He used the word 'passengers' again, and he made it sound like a swear word. In the end, though, he just shrugged, said something that definitely was a swear word and stormed off.

We helped the Ealhams pack up. 'Una will have to travel inside the bus,' Marie said, 'although her ankle's a bit better this morning.'

I was puzzled. 'I thought we'd all be travelling inside the bus.'

'No, love! Only the driver.'

Gene had taken a set of metal shafts from the roof, and was fitting them into holes halfway up the sides of the bus. Harry got into the driver's seat, Una next to him ... and the rest of us took a shaft each and started pushing.

Marie smiled. 'Not quite the romantic life you'd imagined, Dazza?'

I couldn't answer – I was too busy straining to get some purchase on the shaft.

'On the other hand,' she added, 'the good news is, we don't eat children.'

I hoped she couldn't tell I was blushing, since I was already bright red from pushing.

The Ants obviously knew the roads well, because we rarely had to push along narrow ways or uphill. The buses' engines, it turned out, were good for just a couple of hours' powered driving a day, so the Ants only used the solar when it was absolutely necessary – up the steepest climbs, for instance. The rest of the time we pushed: even smaller kids took their turn on the shafts.

We saw no other traffic; we kept off the main roads, which vehicles on official business would use. When we stopped for a tea break midmorning, my arms kept floating upwards of their own accord.

'Sorry about the extra weight on the bus,' said Una.

'Don't worry,' I said, 'if you hadn't talked me into it, we wouldn't be here at all.'

'You pushed well,' Gene told me, as we relaxed on the steps of the bus.

'Thanks,' I said, though I thought he was probably just being kind.

'Whereabouts you trying to get to?'

I showed him Aunty Kath's address. I knew it off by heart, but I'd kept the piece of paper anyway.

'That's not a million miles out of our way,' said Gene. 'Daresay we can drop you near there.'

This brought an angry mutter from Leo, who'd clearly been listening in. He chucked the dregs of his tea on to the verge, and disappeared into his bus.

'Why are Leo and Jan so against us?' I asked.

Gene shrugged. 'He's not keen on strangers, that's all. Sometimes – well, strangers can be dangerous for Ants.'

'Is that why you always keep moving?'

'Partly. The authorities don't much like us. Townspeople get annoyed if we hang around too long in one place.' He grinned. 'But mostly – well, we do it because we can. If you could live in a solar bus with all your family and spend your days travelling the country, wouldn't you?'

I grinned back. 'Yeah! I reckon I would.'


It was hard work, travelling south as a Tinner Ant. But travelling south on our own would have been impossible, and anyway it was different from the hard work of the recycling plant. The days moved to a gentle rhythm, and we took breaks whenever we needed them.

As Una's ankle recovered, so that she could walk with a crutch Harry had cut for her, she'd often go into the woods and forests with Harry and Marie and the children, on foraging expeditions. The Ants had to know a lot about what they called 'fieldcraft' – how to find water and firewood, which mushrooms were poisonous, where to dig for edible roots, what sorts of trees and bushes gave useful fruits or leaves, and which wild herbs could be used as medicines. Even the kids were experts.

From before breakfast until bedtime, there was always plenty to do, and with everyone working together it all got done, without any pressure or panic. It seemed to me a good way of life, and I was sad that, from what Harry had said, it looked like one that wouldn't last much longer.

All the time we were drawing closer to Devon. I began to think that Una and I had at last outrun our troubles. Naturally, I was wrong.

# CHAPTER TWELVE

One night around the campfire, Leo – who was
still having as little as possible to do with me
and Una – said to Marie, 'You do realise we're
going to have to go into Somerset tomorrow, if
we're to drop off your passengers?'

'Only *North* Somerset, Leo.' She sounded
irritated. 'The big military bases are all further
south.'

'Still seems a hell of a risk, just so you can
provide a taxi service for runaways.'

'Well, you don't have to come,' Marie said,
her voice quiet and stern. 'You go on to
Wiltshire, we'll meet you there.'

Leo's head jerked back, as if he'd been
slapped. He stared at her for a moment, his
face reddening, and then he left the fireside
without another word. Nobody else said
anything, either. Marie didn't look at the
others; she stared into the fire, her own face as
red as blood.

Sleep usually came easily after a day spent
pushing a bus, but in bed that night, I fretted.
I was worried that Leo and Marie were worried

about the military bases in Somerset; most of all I was worried by a nasty thought that had been hovering around the back of my mind.

Did Leo hate me and Una enough to turn us in to the authorities? Perhaps he'd even get a reward. Like he said, we *were* runaways.

An hour after lunch, a week or so later, we were crossing the Somerset-Devon border on a twisty, country road. It had been raining and the going was slow. Leo's bus, ahead as usual, was temporarily out of sight around a bend when I heard men shouting, and the sound of engines.

'Ambush!' yelled Gene. He banged his fist against the bus. 'Harry – reverse!'

I heard the engine cough and groan, and Harry called out. 'Nothing! We used up all the stored power on that big hill this morning – you'll have to push. And push hard!'

There was no room to turn the bus, so we all ducked under our shafts and began pushing the vehicle backwards, Harry steering via the rear-view mirror. Una scrambled out of the cab window, and clung on to the roof, shouting directions, 'Left a bit, Harry – left!'

I called up to her, 'You'll fall!'

'Shut up and keep pushing,' she called back.

I asked Marie, on the shaft ahead of mine, what was going on. 'It's soldiers,' she said, panting. 'Or maybe a local militia. They're after the solar panels.'

I understood then one reason why there were so few Ants left: because they had something other people wanted. Just like the people in other countries, forced to export their water ...

'Down there!' Gene shouted, gesturing towards a muddy farm track. 'Army trucks won't be able to follow us down that, they're too big.'

'They'll follow us on foot,' said Marie.

'Maybe, but we can't keep reversing forever.'

We manoeuvred the bus on to the mud track, expecting the trucks to arrive behind us any moment. A little way down the track, we could at last see, over a low hedge and across a field, Leo's van and two military trucks. Jan and her children were standing, arguing with three soldiers. I couldn't spot Leo.

'Good man,' Marie panted. 'See how he's parked it across the road – they'll have to shift it before they come after us.'

'*Fire!*'

We all looked up in horror, only to see that Una was pointing at Leo's bus – not ours. She was right – flames were climbing out of the windows on to the roof, as if trying to escape. The soldiers were hastily withdrawing their trucks, taking Leo and his family with them.

'Why are the soldiers burning his bus?'

'They're not.' Gene sighed. 'Leo is – to distract them.'

Underfoot, the going was getting worse. The ground was too soft to get a proper grip. 'If we get stuck here, they'll catch us anyway,' said Marie.

I tried to push even harder, but there was no doubt now – the bus was slowing down.

'Shift up, Dazza!' Una was next to me; she nudged me along, and grabbed hold of the shaft. All of us strained against the weight of the stalled bus. We kept slipping, losing our hold in the drizzle and banging our knees along the ground. I was soon bruised all over, and wincing at every movement, but Una – with her ankle still not properly healed – was sobbing with pain. Every time she slipped, she howled out, and tears ran like rain down her face. I wanted to tell her to stop, to give up, but I didn't dare. And then, finally, the bus lurched forward, so suddenly that we almost fell under it, and we were moving again.

No campfire that night.

We'd kept pushing for hours, stopping only once, when Una fainted – from pain or exhaustion or both – and then only long enough to bundle her into the bus. At dusk we'd pushed the bus as far as we could into the cover of an isolated copse and swept away our tracks with fir branches. Gene was up a tree, keeping sentry. The rest of us were inside the bus, eating cold rations.

Harry sat down next to me, holding a map.

I could guess what he was going to say.

'It's time for us to part company, isn't it?'

'Yes, lad. I'm sorry.'

'Not your fault, Harry.'

He unfolded the map over both our knees. 'We reckon you're a day's good march from your aunt's farm. Here, see?'

Una and I studied the map hard; they didn't have a spare copy.

'Leo thought we might be spies, didn't he?' I asked, because it had been on my mind even while we were pushing the bus. 'That we were leading you into an ambush.'

Harry nodded. 'In fairness, lad, it has been known to happen.'

Una said, 'So why did you and Marie and Gene pick us up?'

'Because,' he said, quite slowly, 'if you behave all the time as if the worst's going to happen, then the worst has happened, and you might as well pack up.'

'Why was everyone so upset the other night,' I asked, 'when Marie said Leo didn't have to come with us to Devon?'

'She said a bad thing there,' Harry replied, 'and she's sorry for it. Ants travel together, we don't split up. Otherwise we're just ... wanderers. That's why Leo sacrificed his bus to let us get away – because Tinner Ants stick together, no matter what.'

'What'll you do now?'

He looked surprised by the question. 'We'll keep going! You haven't lost until you give up.'

'Is that the Tinner Ants' slogan?' said Una.

'It's not a slogan,' said Harry, sharply. 'It's a simple statement of fact.'

In the morning, Marie gave us each a bag containing water and some bread and apples.

'Where will you go?' Una asked.

'We'll head back up north for a while, until the soldiers have forgotten us. Then sneak back, see if we can find Leo and Jan.'

Una, with cuts all over her face and hands and her eyes still red from the previous day, said, 'Why does everything have to be so *hard*?

Everyone fighting each other over scraps of old machines and water and everything?'

'I don't know, love.'

'I just wish there was something we could do to make a *difference*,' I said.

Marie smiled. 'Ah, well. You ask old Harry, and he'll tell you – everything a human being does makes a difference. You can't avoid it. What sort of difference – that's what you have to decide, and you have to decide that every day of your life.' She stopped and laughed at herself. 'Oh dear, I must be getting old – I sound just like my mother!'

She kissed us both, and we walked off into the copse.

We started just after sunrise, keeping well away from main roads, and it was late afternoon before we reached the outskirts of the village where my aunt had her farm. We'd learned enough to approach cautiously.

'Should be just over there,' I said, seeing in my mind the section of map I'd memorised. 'Once we're clear of these trees, we should be able to see the farmhouse.'

Una put her arm through mine. 'So what

are we waiting for?'

I hadn't realised I'd stopped walking. I tried to smile at her, and she tried to smile back at me, but we were both too nervous for our smiles to be convincing.

What if my parents weren't there? What if Aunty Kath wasn't there? She could have moved, or died, or ...

'Come on,' said Una. 'We've travelled the length of Britain. A few more steps won't kill us.'

*I'm not so sure*, I thought, but I walked on, anyway.

As soon as we emerged from the trees, we could see a stone house with outbuildings in a slight valley beneath us, just across from some fields of corn. I started to say, 'Look, there's a farmhouse,' but Una interrupted, pointing at a field to the left of the house.

'People!' she said. 'A man and a woman, pulling up weeds.'

Even from that distance I knew them: by the way they moved, or by the outlines of their bodies, or – well, somehow I knew them.

Mum and Dad.

As we watched, a big mongrel dog leapt up at my father, and he laughed and pushed it away. It leapt up again so he drew back his arm and pretended to throw a stick as far as he could. Bouncing with joy, the daft dog chased after the non-existent stick, barking its head off.

'Una, did I ever tell you about my dog – the one that wasn't killed when our house got bombed?'

I didn't wait for her answer. I set off running as fast as I could, down the slope and across the field towards my parents and our new home, shouting all the time at the top of my voice. I had to keep stopping for Una to catch up with me. It took them ages to hear me. But they heard me in the end.